DOUBLE MAJOR: FALLING & FAILING

CONTENTS

To the girl I was before,

I've completed your dream.

It's time to wake up.

Freshman Year

Red Lines

In between the red lines.

Sits water pulling at my feet.

Sounds of a faucet are beginning to leak.

Words to others criticizing and analyzing my actions,

until I make a mistake.

Slipping,

Begins a water slide of doubt.

Of others forcing me to drown.

Losing Myself.

Drowning was supposed to be peaceful.
Your mind goes numb,
then your limbs.
As if you're submerged in the freezing ocean.
Unable to move from the pillow of seaweed.
Static.
Stuck.
Lost.
Am I afraid?

Should I be?

Busy Thoughts..

Do you ever wonder..
That you pass millions of people you'll never see again.
You passed me,
You looked down,
You're one of the millions.
You don't know who I am.
Neither do I.

Acid Reflux

Stuff it down.
Suppress it over
and over.

You scream so loud inside your own head.
Till it burns.
Till it burns so much to where,

You feel nothing.

Through The Haze

Through the haze sits a little girl.
There on a tree stump in the distance.
The ignorance of the world around her.

How dare she?

How dare she…
Be allowed to enjoy the subtleties
and not worry about hate.
Not worry about fear.
Not worry about love.

For it is her world.
Her vision.
Her life.

Chocolate Almonds

Covered in a thin shell,
one easily melted away.
They melt as easily as my heart
and perplex my brain.
The shell is temporary.
Cracks with every blow,
Till in the end I am laid out below.

No shell. No protection.
Chocolate almonds.

Write

Write a journal.
Write a book.
Write your life.
With every passing second.
With pride and a rhyme.
Write such that it appeases the soul
and the writing will be left behind
once you turn your back to go.

Letting Go

Our love was different.
I thought it was secure.
I thought it was safe.
I couldn't have been more wrong.
You were like a father scolding a young child.
I learned my lesson over and over and over.

Yet I still hold on to the feeling.
The feeling of disclosing everything to someone
who I thought listened.
Yet half of what I said was always wrong.
I changed to please, until I didn't know if I was
the best version of myself
or someone completely different.

I was unrecognizable.

Do I miss him?
Do I miss his touch?

Do I miss his large shoulders that swallowed me whole?

Why would I miss him?
I still don't know.
Why does a knife feel as if it's plunging into my back
whenever I say his name.

I was replaceable.
He wasn't.

I didn't grieve - I moved on.
Or so I thought.
I decided not to recognize the harsh feelings for a long time.

His time is up in my mind.
This is the letter I write.

No matter what you did.
No matter what you said.
No matter how you feel.

I still love you.

Jam

Am I angry?

Yes

I grow just for YOU to pick the berries.
YOU mash them into jam.
Smack a label on the jar.

YOU turn healthy love and fruit into,
Deceit,
Lies,
Jealousy,
Hypocrisy,
Hate.

I hate that you have chosen hate.
I will not bear more fruit.

Summer
2023

Bleach

Negativity...
Seething…
For an opportunity
Cultivating like bacteria on a petri dish
The bacteria in my mind grows
And grows
And grows

Bleach….
Bleach my brain if only to rid it from the bacteria,
even if it's no longer able to function

Clarity
The nothingness is as good as Novocaine.
Numb and no longer afraid.

Promise?

I'm free now.
I'm free from what hurt me.

Why can't I let it go?
It's been a month.
You're free.

Maybe I'm not.
I have to return to what hurt me.

I'm suffocating.

You have three years left, it'll be okay I promise.

You promise? That's supposed to be enough?
You promised I'd be safe.
You promised I'd be protected.
You promised you'd take care of me.
Your promise was telling me I needed therapy.

You broke me, you can't tell me how to fix me.

Freshman year: Complete
Sophomore year: ...

Yearning

I paint a picture in my mind.
My face gently kissed by the rays of the sun.
Alone and in complete serendipity.
That is what my soul yearns for.
That is what my soul *needs.*

For One Night

I didn't expect you to be mine ever,
let alone one night.
You were perfect.

Memento Mori
to the boy
who made me love again.

Bodies pressed together, lips concealed
Moving together with the sound of music.
I felt as if nothing was real.

It was like a fever dream,
but the taste of your lips was real
My arms draped over your shoulders -
your hands all over me.
The look in your eyes was all I was ever going to need.

Cosmic Meeting

I don't know your story.
You don't know mine,
somehow, we managed to collide
A gift from the universe.
I will remember in every verse.
You are a free spirit.
Your carefree smile and kind eyes.
I will remember forever throughout time.

Italy

I like to have things planned.
Long term -
Short term -
Planned perfection.
But isn't there beauty in imperfection?
That beauty is incomparable.
Bask in it.
Thrive in it.
Most importantly...
Live in it.

Tinder Poems 101

Dark hair,
brown eyes,
kinda crazy, he's just my type.

You like weird girls,
you won't find anyone weirder than me.
Let's continue to grow this family tree.

Overflow

Do you no longer enjoy the things you used to?
Check

Do you struggle with food as in
eating too little or overeating?
Check

Do you….
Check
Check
Check

A list of symptoms does not prove your pain.
My pain.
You released the stress...
Why can't you release the sadness?
Am I grieving the death of who I used to be?

I used to be carefree,
I used to be dedicated,
I used to be grounded,

I used to be
me.

When did I allow other people to change me?

The water builds behind a beaver dam.
One crack and it overflows.
You do not have to put the walls back on your own.
You don't have to bear the pain in the valley of darkness.
Your kindness is not a weakness.
It's a blessing.

Be the blessing, not the darkness.

Moments Of Peace

A calm day but not a calm mind.
A raging night is where I find my peace.
My piece of paradise with a knife and a pistol
stitched to my side.
The night is when I'm no longer alone.
Where my dark thoughts and intentions begin
to hide.
Because in the night, is where I've found my *light*.

My Spark

Be the spark..
I was the spark.
You hated that spark.
Why?

You took it away from me like flowers from a grave.
Your darkness consumed my soul, trapped inside a dark set of jaws.
The jaws do more than talk; they bite.
Eating away at who you are until you're unrecognizable.

My sanctuary

You recognized the real me sealed away.
Your spark gave my wick hope.
Now all I have to do
is **burn.**

Old Me

There is no old me..
There's just me.
I was a shell of a body,
insides torn out and discarded.
Over time…
Just like crumpled paper, my insides were stuffed back in like a Build-A-Bear.
So fearful of hurting others I hurt myself.
At least this time, I don't have to force a smile.
There is no old me.
There's just me….

Connected

There's so many reasons to say no,
and yet,
why do I want to say yes?

Admiration
Determination
Affixation
Magnetization

You may truly only exist,
in my dreams.

Game

Raised with high expectations..
Whether it's socially, athletically, or scholarly.
The highest achievable possibility.
I want that for myself as much as my parents,
but the game I'm playing requires mistakes.
Mistakes are a reminder that I'm not perfect -
I'm human.
But sometimes that's a foreign concept.
When you're the "*perfect daughter.*"

Forgiving Yourself

In my mind is a scared little girl,
broken and hurt.
This little girl questions her worth -
her purpose.
An older girl reaches out and grasps the little girl's hand,
pulling her into herself.
This little girl is a part of you.
She doesn't need to be hidden,
when she is screaming
to be seen.

Just Add H_2O

Water rushing down my back
and down my body,
makes me feel connected and grounded
to this beautiful planet.
I wanted to be a shadow,
left alone - to be on my own.
Now I've found growth,
looking to attract positivity and love.
Like water loves water.
Love loves love.

Sophomore Year

(transferred)

The Phone

I am kind.
Or at least I try to be,
but don't be confused if I have no empathy.
Fooled me once haha.
Fooled me twice..

Is it truly my fault?

Intuition ringing, but the feeling of being wanted hung up the
phone.

I got what I wanted, not a night alone.
But that's all I wanted.
Not the leering feeling of you only wanting
one thing and one thing alone.

I made sure you knew that's not what I was about to share, for
it means more
then what you'd have lasted.
I thought you'd last maybe a semester
not less than 24 hours

The mark you left lasted longer than your name on my tongue.
For if meeting me didn't mean anymore to you
you could've just left me alone.
But instead, you decided
to pick up - *the phone.*

Reminders

The haze wakes through the forest and eases its way into the mind.
The haze sits as if a note on the piano is pressed for an eternity.
The haze is the music playing between each memory.

The memory is almost haunting.
It was the beginning of something that was never meant to end.
But it needed to.
If it didn't,
you would have.

Thank You

Thank you.
For treating me,
like the gum you spit out of your mouth.
Like the weights you let slam into the gym floor.
Like the worst person you ever met.
Like my existence hindered yours so.

Treating me so,
I believed that it was me.
Who had to change.

Rooted

Slouched down in sorrow,
my mind refuses to wander about tomorrow.
My back is strung into the past with a tight coarse rope.
Pulling. Tugging.
The rope is knitted around my spine.
The rope is being pulled. - Pulled by who? - You ask. - Yourself.
Just like that dagger that you so love that you had placed in a moment of violence against your soul,
the rope will keep pulling and pulling until you decide to drop the rope and walk away.
Release the rope. Remove the dagger.
Remind yourself you are doing better.
Be kind to your own mind just like speaking positive affirmations to a soon to be gorgeous flower.
The roots are brown and tangled up.
The rope is brown and tangled up.
Just like the flower will bloom, so will you.

J.

The childhood bliss of warmth growing on my cheeks.
The very same bliss absent for years,
Somehow, discovers me at 18.
Somehow, *you* did too.

Balance

I shared a piece of my heart with all of you.
Protect that piece.
In hopes that eventually,
I'll be able to share more too.

Collectively, together, we will be able to piece together
a miraculous masterpiece.
Our pieces do not look the same, but we all go together
to make something,
no other pieces can ever create.

Self Sabotage

I'm nervous.
I'm nervous to lose you, when I've only just gotten you.
I'm nervous that my thoughts will spiral till I am unsure of what to think, what to feel, what to say.

My thoughts love to interrupt when I finally feel happy.
As if that's not an emotion I should be allowed to feel anymore.
If I'm transparent, will that make it easier?
Or will it be just as damaging to admit out loud?
If I overthink, I can damage everything.

But this itself is an overthinking thought,
Me inserting emotions onto a screen,
So my heart and brain no longer has to bleed.

B&W

There is no such thing as simply black and white.
The world is filled with shades of gray.
I live in a world of gray.
Painting and highlighting the most fascinating features,
into a million scales of gray sent from a dragon's back.

There is power in the gray.
If only you understand it.
Light in darkness is very demanding.
Lighting the world slowly.
Until it is snuffed out.
Then there is no gray.
No black and white
Just…
Absence of life.

Funny

Isn't it funny.

Isn't it funny that you're relearning what you thought
you knew about the world,
about everything,
about yourself?
It's funny, isn't it?
Isn't it funny that I lost the very critical factors
that makes me whole.
Is it funny I have to ask myself who I am?
Who I'm supposed to be?
I knew who I was.

Who am I now?

Seasonal

Fall is my favorite season.
The sunsets feel gentle on lightly chilled skin.
Sweaters of variety and leggings enough to keep my body warm.

As earth turns, fall falls as quick as an avalanche into the winter.
The sweaters turn into hoodies and sweatpants
and my head falls into a quieter place like sound absorbed
by the snow that traces the ground.
It gets quiet and the sun doesn't dare to whisper.

The sun disappearing is a betrayal to my soul.
Wandering freely into a darker,
sadder place without the light to draw it out.

I fall with fall.
Tis the season.

Palatable

Darkness is sort of beautiful.
It's this meticulous thing.
It's able to consume fractions of light in an instant.

Swirling around emotions on a palette,
Each emotion now fully emerged into depression.
Exactly how all colors are absorbed by the color black.

The remedy for such a thing is to add white.
Although it takes 10x maybe even 100x the amount to make
the darkness lighten up again.

Once the light is added then the emotions,
each within their own retrospect can be added once again.

Anger,
Sadness,
Joy,
Happiness,
Excitement,

Slowly the pallet can rebuild,
but it will take much longer than if a singular drop of black is added.

Unlike our human minds
A soiled blacked palette once filled with an array of color, can be simply - washed off.
The colors, then added back on - renewed.

Our mind can never be wiped off and made a fresh slate.
We can continue to remedy it with white and add some color back but we will always be left with some gray,
and that gray... well...
we simply have to learn to live with it like we never have lived without.

Our pallets.

Feel

Feelings.

How am I allowed to feel?
When growing up it was always,
don't cry,
don't get emotional,
don't let it get to you.

Don't let it get to me?
I didn't,
but now... I don't feel.

Why am I so afraid to feel any emotion that's not happiness?
When I haven't felt true happiness without pain in months.

I go to cry, and as soon as I hear footsteps,
I wipe my tears,
check my voice, and fake a smile.
For if they see me crying, they won't understand what is wrong with me.
And I don't want my mother to even think it's her fault.

That's worse than the pain itself.

Every Moon

There are so many sounds that bless this planet,
Many people and creatures
with their very own pitch and tune.
Each falls into a complex rhythm in which we are consumed.

Consuming my mind, my absolute favorite tune,
Is your lovely laugh, every moon.
I love your laugh and all of you.
I want to be consumed forever in awe of you.

That Girl?

You know that girl.
The girl that gets pushed away,
The girl that walks in the grass so the others can walk beside each other on the sidewalks.
The girl that listens intently
to every word that comes out her friend's mouths,
only to be silenced when she opened hers.

You know that girl?
Don't you?
The girl that put both of your needs above her own.
The girl that thought she was finally needed.
The girl that wanted a best friend, something she could never have.
The girl that got used as a therapist when the two refused to get along.
The girl whose wallet was always rummaged through to help her "friends" get a dinner they couldn't afford.

That girl.
She gave so much to the two of you.

Gave everything.

I'm Barbie

Barbie.
Gymnastics Barbie,
Fitness Barbie,
Mermaid Barbie,
Perfect Barbie,

Oh wait.
They're all perfect.

This Barbie in particular is not.
This Barbie is emotionless but flooding
with overwhelming emotions at the same time.
This Barbie is not plastic but you can braid her hair.
She'll change her own clothes and travel anywhere.
Traveling is a distraction beyond compare.

If only this Barbie,
could braid her own hair.

Vice

People depend on various vices to produce happiness in
their brains for a limited amount of time.
Vices include alcohol, hard drugs, girls, boys, and plenty others.
I'd like to think I was your vice.

I gave you happiness in doses until my doses weren't enough.
I noticed my doses in return weakened but it didn't matter.
You were more than a vice to me.
I'd pick you a million times over.

You just wouldn't choose me.

True Love

I loved the idea of love many times.
The idea of love led to many relationships where I ended them
because they didn't matter.

The end goal wasn't in sight back then.
The idea of love taught me who I would want to love me
and who I would love for all an eternity.
Eventually, the idea of love wasn't what I was in love with
- it was him.

The boy who always effortlessly smiled and
could light up the whole room.
The boy who could make any phrase a funny trend
to last for weeks on end.
The boy who was the fifth who wanted the sixth.
The boy that I finally lent my heart and soul to.
The boy I will always love.

If One Would Sing

Fires up, fires down.
Who knew how much I could rage within the crowd.
Fires up, fires down.
What I wouldn't do to put it out.

Rain oh rain oh rain.
Let the water fall
Down down down,
Down down,
Down until you drown.

Fade - fade - fade away.
Into the ashes in your grave.

5 Days

It's been five days.

Five days since,
I've heard your laugh,
my favorite sound in the world.

Five days since,
I've been touched by you,
my favorite feeling in the world.

Five days since,
I've felt seen by you,
my favorite eyes to gaze into.

Five days since,
Five days.
Five.
It's been..
Five...

Enough

" I never told you about past me "

I didn't know your past you.
That alone is true.

But I love present you and will love who you were and
who you will grow to be.

Your aloud to grow and to reflect on your own life.

You were enough before you met me and
will always continue to be enough.

Know that.

You are precious.
You are loved.
You are everything.

You deserve the universe and then some.
If only I could be the one to give it to you.

Forest

You were addicting like the trees and
the fresh forest air.
You were light in my heart like the
animals dancing in the very same forest.
The addiction to this forest soon became overgrown.
The trees piled on each other till they couldn't
even intake oxygen between their leaves.
Leaving a rotted land once filled with love
and the feeling of being set free.

Stuck

Continuing to love you or deciding to stop loving you.
Is the hardest decision I have ever made.

A decision - I have yet to make.

I want to love you, but only if it's requited.
I do not want to wait and love you from a distance to one day
see you gaze into a different girl's eyes -
the exact way you did mine.

But.
I want to always love you.
I want everything with you.
That was the decision I made.

Before you were even mine.

Weights

There's something wrong my body tells me.
My body tells me through shaking hands,
And a blood rush when I have the weight of my world among my shoulders.
My body is telling me, screaming at me something's wrong.

If only I knew how to fix it.

Scared

You're scared about what I would write?
Really?
You're scared?
Of me?
Of what could be?
Of what could've been?
To even talk to me?

Are you scared to feel something you chose to try to forget?
Only to find out you were wrong?

You're scared.
That's okay.

I'll wait.

Waiting is what scares me.
Just like I scared you.

Shadow Of A Woman

Hi, I'd like to make an appointment please.
Why does it make me feel worthless?

Once again, water pulling between my feet.
Between scattered lines and new brick walls.
A shadow of a girl yanking.
Dragging.

A girl who should've been released,
yet her chains still locked tightly on her ankles and her neck.
Locking her in place.

A girl who was temporarily forgotten - but is demanding
to be remembered.

"Hi"

Hi!
You jump straight up telephone pole tight.
Huh.
I still scare you?
I didn't think "Hi" was scare worthy.
After all.
We're not really strangers.
A simple "Hi" shouldn't make you jump out of your own skin.
Especially when your eyes wander to me.
You look, but are afraid to speak.
What demons are you fighting?
If only you could let me see.

Deeper you fall into my memory.

Conditioned

She was conditioned to be afraid.
She was conditioned to be sad.
She was conditioned to be lost.
Seeking her past self that was forever locked away.
She was conditioned this way because her smile
and love out-shined the hatred around her.
Until they conditioned her to hate too.

High

A heart can be indistinguishable the most
intricate piece of a human physically and metaphorically.
"Wear your heart on your sleeve."
Is it on my sleeve so it's easier to break?
Instead of shelled in like prison bars on my chest?
My heart has been given out over the years.
When will I run out?
The wounds that leak me dry.
Blood seeps through the bandages.
Stitches burst open with every breath.
I heal others' wounds without paying mind to my own.
The high of healing someone else.
Is worth dying for.

Not To

Trying not to love you is like trying not to breathe.
It has this constant repetitive influx to stay alive.
Because my soul became intertwined now it's so tangled
I can't weave myself out even with saw blades
 bigger than a whole forest by itself.
I don't want stuck forever,
but I don't want to lose the beauty in the disaster.
Because we created this disaster,
it is now ours to lose.

Left Unsent

I still love you..
I still want you..
Regardless if you want me.
I just know that it was true for a time.
If only that time was for eternity.

How Much?

What I'm willing to tell you?
The answer was everything.
Now there's a little wall sectioned off.
That wall is protecting myself from the forever ruins
I'm afraid it will turn out to be.
But I want to be able to tell you.
Tell you how much it hurt.
How much I've ached.
How much I've cried.
How much I've wished I was enough.
How much I wished you were ready.
How much I wished to God for you to be mine.

You came that night, you both heard me.
But will you answer your heart or your mind?
Something so intricate I would be forced to hide.
If the stars light up at night, I still find comfort
that we are forever under the same sky.

Safe Space

You were my safe space.
What calmed my fears and racing thoughts.
Now when I dream of wrapping my arms delicately
around your neck.
I only get the touch of empty air.
My arms need to be taught to be wrapped around myself.
I need to be my own safe space.
My own sanctuary.
Then my arms can wrap around millions of others
and be their safe space too.

Eye Contact

I know you feel it.
I know you feel it cause I felt it too.
Rooted deep inside of me.
Looking into the void of one another.
It's a familiar darkness that only we can bring light to.

Self Preservation

"Soon this will all become a memory."
The joy.
The sadness.
The life lessons.
But for now, it's my present reality.
A reality I wish to change for the better.
I cannot run away this time.
I have to grow roots that grant me stability and strength.
To build something of my own accord.
Even if it's without water.

Stone Worker

You soon will cause me to turn into stone.
For stone has no ambitions
but maintains structure.
And structure is my singular contribution
for what else I have to offer
is simply too little for any discernment from you.

Notice

Whenever being asked
"how are you?"
Becomes to hard to simply answer.

Caged

"Talking solves everything"
If you're talking to the right person.
Never apologize for how you feel.
Please do not cage your heart in,
I beg of you.
Feel how you feel and feel deeply -
Love deeply.
Your capacity to love is a testament to your soul.
That you are beautiful.
Do not cage yourself in
when you are meant to be free.

Honey

You're expected to crash.
So you do.
You always did what was expected.

Then they fed you excuses.
So, you did then too.

Fed the excuses and lies till expectations were as good as the truth.

Deep inside you knew it was bullshit.
They made you average.
Oh honey…

They put you in a sticky place.
But you're not too sweet to stay there.

More than average.
Bitter than honey.

Another Year

Was it a waste of time?
A waste of a year?
In some aspects of what I desire.
That is completely possible.
Wasted love.
Wasted trust.
Wasted time.
But I did not waste the ability to become a better person.
I will not be wasted on.

Cheers to moving on.

After

"I'm in love with him"
No darling. You're in love with who you thought he was.
He is not your happily ever after.
He is just.
After.

Summer
2024

Hope

Headphones cancel out the world around me.
They bring me to a whole new universe.
A universe I create between the lines -
of music blaring in each ear.
One night, and only just once, headphones weren't needed.
The universe itself pounded with drums
and violins and stars that lit up the night.
Thousands of people became consumed by this black hole.
Reaping freedom for a limited time.
The rush of the newfound universe
will forever be remembered
within his verse.
If the universe's ceiling opens.
Everyone can be consumed,
enthralled,
connected.
If we are connected, we are never truly alone.
If only we open ourselves to the world around us.
The world will welcome us.

Fawn

The touch and gaze of absolute innocence
Light shining through dark fawn lashes.
Birds and other animals watching shortly in the distance.
Causing nature's heartbeat to thrum,
Thrumming faster and faster.
Till an unfamiliar connection caused it to thrum to a complete
stop.
Stunning nature into silence.
Those that recognized the creature for murder,
watched as it became a friend of nature
in complete, utter silence.

Hunch

To the girl who thought her life would end at 16.

You made your senior prom.
Your graduation.
You won states.
You made millions of people happy.
And you're beginning to make yourself happy too.
It was never the question of you taking your own life.
It was the hunch that someone would do it for you.
That same hunch just so happened to save you.

Do not let someone take you from this beautiful planet.
The darkness you hold isn't true to you.
We were meant to survive, and I see a fighter in all of you.

Crescent Seat

My imaginary chains are confining and suffocating.
The most violent and isolating type.
My real chains showed when I was just a girl.
The chains held onto a dark blue crescent seat.
That same seat fit my little body comfortably and safely.
The chains would hold me as I freely swung through the air.
The chains offered me freedom and a sense of relaxation.
At that time, chains were a support that gave me the ability to fly.
The chains allowed me to be free.
These same chains, so inherently depressive to me now, that once fed my childlike mind,
are crippling and dark.

Childhood bliss is fleeting.

Cruel

Nature is cruel.
Something that made nature's heartbeat
come to a complete dead stop
as if it was an amazement,
but instead because a life had come to an end.
Something so sweet and so innocent
that was breathing the fresh forest air, suddenly suffocated.
Undeserving of such a fate.
Innocence never remains unsullied.
All precious things decay eventually.
What's your half-life?
Or simply your life?

Looking Ahead

Writing is like consuming shots and shots of liquor.
Drowning and blacking out my thoughts and feelings.
The more I write, the less I remember,
Until, of course, I reopen my own wounds.
Reading memories I have long forgotten.
Maybe, by reading my memories,
Those you yourself have forgotten will bleed too.
But instead this time, the wounds won't reopen.
The scars will remain, yes.
But the past will no longer swallow you whole,
it will just become part of who you are.
Who you will be.

Mr. Blue

Mr blue shirt.
We didn't ask for your unsolicited words.
Mr blue shirt.
We didn't ask to be sexualized with your prying eyes.
Mr blue shirt.
We didn't want to be crowded in our own little worlds.
Mr blue shirt.
You turn blue as I turn red.
Now you have to forever lie in your own bed.

Forever Red

These poems are my self-harm.
A place where my scars get deeper and darker.
Pieces of my soul will be forever drowned within these pages.

These pages are soaked in tears,
but the ink will run forever red.
A source of symbolism for
a lack of symbiotic action against oneself.
Action others thought she would commit to.

However,
She had never placed a blade on skin
like she has placed
words unto paper.

Made Of Maple

You are the one that always smiles.
That is your staple, let alone that you have always been as sweet as maple.

Sweet as maple turned unstable due to a tap that ran dry.

The tree being ageless amongst time was told that the syrup would come within the next hour.
All refused to aid the tree for it has always been easily devoured.

Many doubted the tree needed aid.
Many even ridiculed the tree whenever it began to aid itself.

The tree reopened a new tap.
Not quite as sweet and as strong before but still made of maple.

Life continued as if the tree never ran dry.
No one acknowledging its rusted tap that still remained.
As long as she is made of maple.

The others will forever remain the same.

SOS

The giants and dragons admire the lights below.
Like we humans admire the stars above.

An encroachment in the sky threatening to quickly
gobble it up.

Stealing the little stars like souls that pass below.
The cycle will continue as the wind forever blows.

My Love Language

Indescribable.
However, I can describe you.
But not quite how I feel about you.

The way I look at you is how I look at the night sky.
You are a star that captivates me.
The best part is,
I want you to.

Self Doubt

I doubt.
Because if I never imagine the happiness it could bring me,
I won't have to grieve it when it's gone.

My doubt kills excitement, but is
constantly met with self-reassurance.
I'm smarter to know that I have no reason to feel that way.
But my brain and my heart do not feel the same way.

My doubt keeps walls built, but my feelings try to break them down.
And hopefully, when the dust settles.
Self-doubt will no longer be around.

Authority

Belittled.
Be little.
Being made to feel small.

The feeling that was projected of shadows drowning your self-worth into themselves to make them stronger.

A sense of power that feeds the ego like an animal searching for its next meal.
Cunning and deceiving.

I will not let you sink your teeth into me.
For I refuse to feed into a man's fantasy of where he has power over me.

Peace

A deep breath and a long look at the stars
is my favorite prescription.
A prescription not prescribed by doctors but by my own soul.
My whole being is entranced in space
as some of me must be star matter in itself.

Inhale.
Pause.
Exhale.

Did you feel that?

Star Dust

The night sky is so forgiving.
I can be laid bare down to my bones,
and the starlight will continue to dance
among my very own skin.
Briskly and beautifully.
The night makes the imperfect...
Perfect.
During the day, when the sun hides the moon,
imperfect is well - not perfect
That much is true,
-however-
Each minor detail makes up a part of you.
The minor details are made up out of star dust and,
you shine perfectly,
your own incredible hue.

Junior Year

Not After Butterflies

The thought of chasing butterflies was appealing to the tiny girl.
Fun and fast and terribly difficult even with her little blue net.
It was indeed fun but it could never last.
As the tiny girl grew into a young beautiful woman
she came to the realization that it was not butterflies she was after.
The young woman stopped chasing.
No longer in search of a pursuit that made her stomach turn into knots.
She craved peace.
Peace that she found looking at the stars or listening to the ocean waves.
She never truly thought she would find peace in someone's eyes.
His presence is calming like the stars and a gentle love
like the small rippling waves of the sea.
From the earth to the sky,
peace is in his eyes.

Confidence

A trigger.
Not the firm metal or plastic one.
But a word.
Growing up, words meant little to me from those who did not
care to know me.
Words that were meant to be hurtful.
Now a singular word meant in pure intentions.
Breaks into my mind, surrounded in silence.
That word gets louder and stronger each time it weaves its
way into my head.
The word slowly lets other thoughts chime in, quietly, at first,
but then each grew louder than the last,
until my ears went deaf and my eyes shot blanks.
Who knew one little word.
Could tear down a powerful woman.

It's been 2 years since it wasn't truly myself
holding the trigger to my head.

My Poem Book

I write poems.
Yes that is true.
I've strayed from my ink after finding my favorite hue.
A hue of green with the occasional hint of blue.
My poems became words,
Spoken to you.

Tea

You knew this was coming?
Why can't you see?
Some will never change, even after three.
It starts with disdain and ends fleetingly.
Parents try to strangle and mangle my favorite cup of tea.

Forcing me away, the leaves steep too long
and turn too bitter
and the taste becomes too strong.

My favorite teacup is still complete
but the tea inside is a wasteland you see.
My only remedy is to pour it down the drain and wipe the teacup clean,
For my parents made it too bitter,
even for me.

Face The Sun

Shadows can amplify if you let them,
Nature leaves them behind you for a reason,
Allow yourself to leave them there.
In the light,
is where we belong.

With The Power Of Friendship

A hot steamy room is one she'd rake
through her sorrows in,
at least it's a bath and
not a car turned on
inside trapping herself in.
Steam renews life, wiping the slate clean,
while caving in internally is an infinite disparity.
Forced and propelled to keep moving forward.
With my friends' love I'll make it much farther.

Please.

A cycle.
Same result, different lesson.
A fall.
From grace, to disgrace.
A rise.
From devil, to child of God.
A future.
From darkness, to infinite light.
A gift.
From fear of death, to only gain.
A mind.
From despair, to clarity.
A name.
With the ability to quench fear and anxiety.
Call out His name, and you will be saved.

I thought I couldn't be.
Truly.

Shame and guilt can be consuming.
He'll guide you to the light.

Please, don't be afraid to walk in it.

Summer
2025

Backyard Poetry

Sunrise or Sunset?
Sun or the moon?

The Sun says goodbye as the Moon watches her leave,
desperately fleeting on what could be.
A saddend-filled cycle that may never end,
but grants the world colors we will never comprehend.
The orange and red gave way to the Moon,
which in turn gives a special lavender hue.
The Sun goes away, which pulls out our tears,
leaving us with darkness until she reappears.

The Sun's final gift is illuminating our Moon,
and the stars remind us of her promise to return soon.

Fear Is Of The devil

A bird encapsulated in its cage by its metal rusted bars for fear
of the unknown and of the noise outside.
The bird was afraid of "what ifs" and potential dangers,
but on one faithful day, it caught a glimpse
of a million others singing and flying happily.

The bird caught a glimmer of hope and a pinch of courage.
The bird now faces a problem. The cage is locked.

Now determined to break free of the cage,
the bird gathered all its strength and chiseled away at the bars.
Finally its open.
The bird inches its way to the edge, it hesitates,
fear and uncertainty floods over, the bird pauses and
reminds themselves of what is waiting for them beyond,
and begins to fly.
The bird joins with the flock, overjoyed
but filled with self-guilt.

Self-guilt is of the devil.

Self-guilt and anguish plagued the bird,
frustrated with itself for not traveling outside sooner
due to the fear of uncertainty.

After sitting in a wave of misery, the bird practiced gratitude.
It is outside and free now,
and the bird gracefully forgives itself for the past.
With the bird's heart lightened,
it continued to sing and fly and see new places for all its days.

God is grace, peace, forgiveness, and love.

Feel free to ask for it, but don't forget to forgive yourself too.

Not Your Average Love Letter

I have this deep feeling.
My soul and non-worldly being yearns for him,
For our souls to be intertwined in this present world.
Not to be seen as a garden to be plowed and harvested,
but to be nurtured and cared for,
and to grow together in purity and grace of the Lord.

I have this deep, immeasurable feeling.

See you soon.

Love,
Your Future Wife

Senior Year

The Fall

They say every time you replay a memory, it is never the same
-
that it evolves and changes.
Never recalling the same event twice.

I've never quite yearned to keep a memory intact to perfection.
However,
there was bound to be an enigma.

I want to keep that particular memory reliable and
re-playable like an old VHS tape.
One I can rewind and watch over and over without mistaking
the way you spoke,
the way you looked at me, and the way
that you held me.

I'll replay it over and over, to see the very first cornerstone of
where the fall began.

But,

I know that when I do,
You'll catch me.

Aflame

My heart is but a flickering flame.
I'll burn everything,
to keep it warm.

Shelf-Life

Spent 21 years on the shelf.
Injected with millions of preservatives to stay desirable.
I anticipate my sell-by date will be up soon.
If I was a loaf of bread, maybe, just maybe,
I'd be chosen by now.
But instead, I wait as days traverse by, watching other loaves
and fruits being plucked off the shelves.
I'm happy for them.
They were chosen.
But time is running out.
Will I ever be?

Fuel For The Fire

Wandering the building in search of my desired genre.
I went in circles and circles not understanding what I was missing
till I asked an employee where it was located.
If I was in search of fiction.
I'd find a book - instantly.
However, poetry is a different story.
Poetry sections are so short, but I could sit with the books for hours.
Getting the taste of someone else's heart and soul poured onto the pages I hold.
Many hearts are filled with
love and admiration for a man.
My book isn't so far from that either.
But right now, I'm sick of searching for my husband's lips
and his hilarious laugh.
I do not yearn for a book to fill me with hopeless desires of which are love.
I want a cynical approach,
a woman that craves independence and self-finding.
I want to find myself

over and over.

It's time to do it again.
Maybe this time I can stay myself.
Who I want me to be.
Not what the voices and the stares suggest.
My candle was lit but was snuffed out for I forgot to breathe.
I vow to fuel the fire and light a spark myself.
Without doubt I will set it ablaze.
I never thought I'd fight fire with fire.
But this is the one burning building, only I can save myself in.

Toilet Poetry

You'd be surprised at how many poems I've written on the toilet or in the shower.
The bathroom is one of the only places
where you can stop being perceived.
When you're in college,
sometimes that's the only refuge one can obtain.
There's a solace in that.
The bathroom slowly became the place for my private thoughts.
The thoughts I share with you all now.
Some cringey and ironic, and others heartfelt.
My emotions expressed behind the locked door
and the pages you can now read.
Next time you're sitting in the bathroom or showering in silence,
remind yourself that if you need to laugh - laugh
if you want to cry - cry.
The bathroom walls will keep your secret and so will I.

The Real Rapunzel

I can see why people say men marry brunettes and
have fun with the blondes.

Blonde is the sign of a woman's youth.

When I was younger,
I was a brilliant natural blonde.
But as I grew older, my blonde started
getting deeper and darker.
Turning into dirty blonde,
then a brown with highlights then simply a brunette.
Every summer, I wish the blonde back from the sun
for the fun and life of youth.
But it isn't coming back,
so I've learned to love my brunette
and I pray, and I wait,
for someone else to love it too.

Yearn To Be Seen

How can I make them see me like I do.

My heart is freezing back over.
A glistening deep blue heart.
But instead of fearing the cold and curdling inside the deep blue.
My soul is skating and dancing on it freely without restraint.
For when it ices over instead of curling up she will dance.
Dance till her blades dig in till it starts to crack allowing warmth to seep back in.
The blades of her strength will let her breakthrough.
Maybe you'll start to see her just like she wants you to.

I Was Wrong

"Love is ever evolving and changing."
That at the very core, isn't correct.
My heart that's been displayed and dissected
over the last four years by boys who I thought
"loved" me and I "loved" them.
For four years, I missed the point.
I was seeking relationships to fill a void
I didn't know was encapsulating me.
I was suddenly "stable" and "happy"
putting constant effort into relationships
to avoid my true responsibilities
and forgetting myself entirely.
Wasting away for it to grow dim and rotten over time,
bearing no fruit at all.

Love isn't material and it doesn't change.
Love is encapsulating,
warm and forever enduring.
I was searching in the wrong place for something
of my own misunderstanding.

Then it happened.
Warmth ran over my body in song
and tears streamed from my eyes.
The warmth of God surrounding me.
The eternal love promised to me.
God doesn't just help those who are
physically blind to gain sight.
For a child is an eternal student,
and God the Father - the eternal teacher.

B.S.

Idolizing college was a big thing when I graduated high school.
I wanted it to be over so bad back then,
so excited for the new things to come.
Turns out, even after another four years,
the sentiment remains the same.

Unraveling

The brick walls and rolling hills I saw myself in,
faded to black before my eyes.
I had a whole future I could imagine,
and then in a single moment it was gone.
Instead, it was replaced with one I could've
never thought up on my own.
Instead of the finish line in sight, I would see a glance as an
unraveling road at the top of the hill with miles
and more mountains to go.
My future is elusive and a mystery.
However, thankfully, I have gotten to choose who I am
and who I want to be.
I can't wait for the unraveling road to be mapped with pictures
and bright colors of my own driven path,
and hopefully,
I'll pick up a few hitchhikers too.
;)

College Athletics

I forgot what it meant to do things for myself.
My career path wasn't mine to choose,
and my college sport felt that way too.
I used to uproot my whole life when things didn't fit me right,
but this last time I chose to stay.
I was forcing myself to stay rooted in a place
that no longer served me
and only burdened my thoughts continuously.
I forced myself to stay, because I thought I was running -
again.
But now that it's all over, I realize.
I froze and dealt with my stagnant reality.
Instead of having a personal why,
I created a why to keep going,
to maintain a false narrative and complacetness.
The contracts and obligations finally ended,
leaving me with clarity and peace within my quieted mind.

———————

I guess I learned the hard way.
I wish I bought a paper shredder.

Not Bittersweet

This chapter of my life closing isn't quite bittersweet.

However, this girl is still bitter than honey.

And she is still,
made of maple.

About the Author

I was a girl who knew exactly what I was going to do
and how I was going to do it.
After I entered my freshman year of college, all of that
changed.
I started writing because I was forced to be silent.
This book is the journey of losing myself
and trying to rebuild everything I thought I ever knew.

All glass mosaics are made up of broken pieces.
Even if you feel broken, you are still radiating beauty.
Perfection is unattainable — take care of yourself.

Love,

Rose

www.ingramcontent.com/pod-product-compliance
Lightning Source LLC
LaVergne TN
LVHW040520210926
848480LV00007BA/1533
* 9 7 9 8 2 3 4 0 9 1 2 2 2 *